SANCCOB was set up in Cape Town, South Africa, in 1968. Since then, it has treated more than 90,000 African penguins and other threatened seabirds. SANCCOB carries out research to find out how healthy South African seabirds are. It trains zoo keepers, vets and rescue workers from all over the world. SANCCOB staff also talk to people about conservation, which means protecting wild animals in danger.

AFRICAN PENGUINS

SANCCOB does most of its work with African penguins. This bird is also sometimes called the black-footed penguin, because of its black feet, or the jackass penguin, because it brays like a donkey (a jackass is a male donkey).

African penguins live and breed on islands off the southern coast of Africa. They have a special way of coping with the heat. They send more blood to the pink patches above their eyes. The blood loses some of its warmth to the air, and this keeps the penguins cool!

CONTENTS

SAVING SEABIRDS

The southern tip of Africa is home to a very special organisation, the Southern African Foundation for the Conservation of Coastal Birds (SANCCOB). Its rescue centre looks after seabirds, especially endangered species such as the African penguin.

The SANCCOB staff and volunteers collect eggs that have been abandoned (left behind) by seabirds. They keep them warm until they hatch, and then look after the chicks. SANCCOB workers also find and rescue seabirds that are ill or injured. They care for them until they are strong and healthy again. Then they can be rehabilitated – prepared for a return to the wild.

In 1910 there were around 1.5 million African penguins. Today, there are only 50,000 or so. They are endangered, which means there is a risk African penguins may become extinct. In order to survive, the penguins need safe places to breed, enough food to eat and clean seas to live in.

Fact File: Changing Threats

Until the early 1900s, the two big threats to African penguins were egg collectors taking their eggs for food, and guano (poo) collectors taking their poo for fertiliser. African penguins need their poo as they use it to make their nests. Today, it is illegal to collect eggs or guano from African penguins.

7

CHICK RESCUE

The South African government has made laws to protect the places where African penguins breed. They are nature reserves. The staff and volunteers at SANCCOB work with the wardens who look after the reserves.

Penguins live in groups called colonies. There is an important colony at Stony Point Nature Reserve. The warden walks around the reserve every day. He keeps track of the chicks' health. He can tell which chicks are growing fat and fluffy, and which are not, just by looking. He also takes measurements.

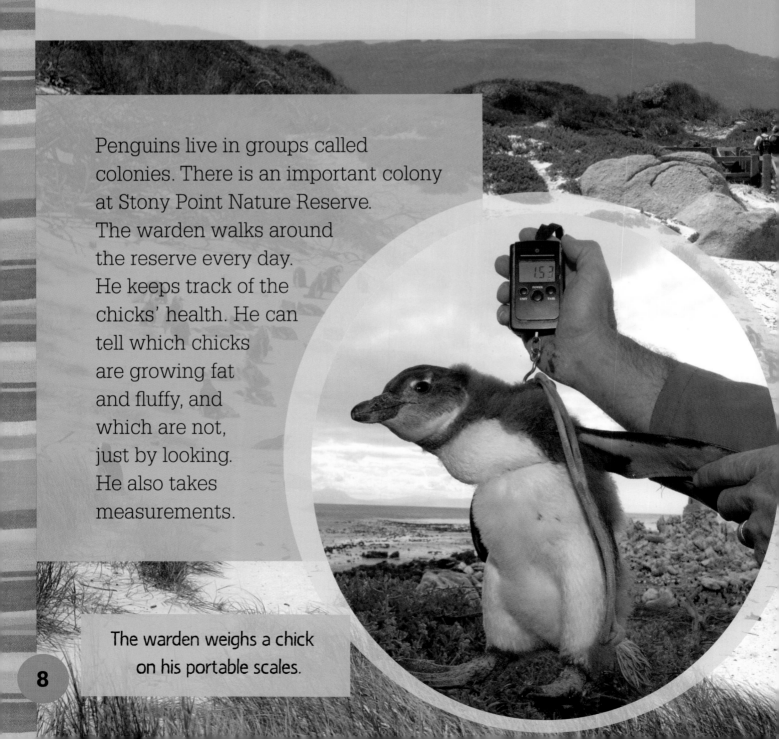

The warden weighs a chick on his portable scales.

If a chick is not putting on weight, its parents have probably abandoned it. This is most likely to happen late in the breeding season, if the parents start to moult (lose their feathers) before their chicks can fend for themselves. Moulting penguins cannot swim, so they cannot catch fish to feed their chicks. The warden sends any abandoned chicks to SANCCOB's rescue centre.

ON ARRIVAL

At the rescue centre, the team are ready and waiting to look after the abandoned chicks. The birds are often dehydrated (in need of water), so the staff use a syringe to squirt fluids into the birds' beaks. After that, the chicks are examined carefully.

Each chick is weighed and checked for injuries or signs of illness. The chicks are tagged so that they are easy to identify (recognise) from now on. Next, they are given an injection of vitamins to help kick-start their recovery. They are also dusted with a special powder that kills off any parasites in their feathers. Parasites are small creatures that live on a larger creature.

Fact File: Penguin Patients

The penguins are wild animals, so they are naturally scared of their human helpers. The staff all wear gloves, but they still get nipped and bruised! They don't mind, though. They know that the pluckiest penguins are the ones with the best chance of survival.

The staff settle the birds into their new home. Larger birds are put in pens. Chicks go into the Chick Rearing Unit (CRU) unless they need specialist care. If so, they start out in the Intensive Care Unit (ICU) instead.

DAILY ROUTINE

The rescue centre treats around 2,500 seabirds a year, and most are African penguins. If there is a disaster such as an oil spill, SANCCOB rescues even more. Looking after the birds is a tough round-the-clock job.

The penguins at the rescue centre have a carefully planned daily routine. It is the best way for the staff to be sure that each bird receives the care it needs. The birds must be fed and hydrated (given drinks) all day and all night. Some penguins may have breathing difficulties or infections. They need medicines, such as antibiotics or special ointments.

For the birds in the pens, swimming is an important part of the daily routine. The birds from each pen have their own time in the pool. The penguins must practise their swimming skills and increase their strength. Once they are released back into the wild, they will need to catch their own food to survive. They need to be strong to dive for squid and fish.

DINNER TIME

In the wild, African penguins dive for their dinner out in the open water. They need more than 540 g (1.2 lb) of food a day. They feed on pilchards, anchovies and other fish. They also hunt squid and small crustaceans (shelled sea creatures).

At the rescue centre, the penguins cannot feed themselves. Their human helpers have to help them, even though the penguins do not always trust them and sometimes spit out the food. The helpers feed the penguins with sardines and pilchards. They feed the weakest birds fish drinks.

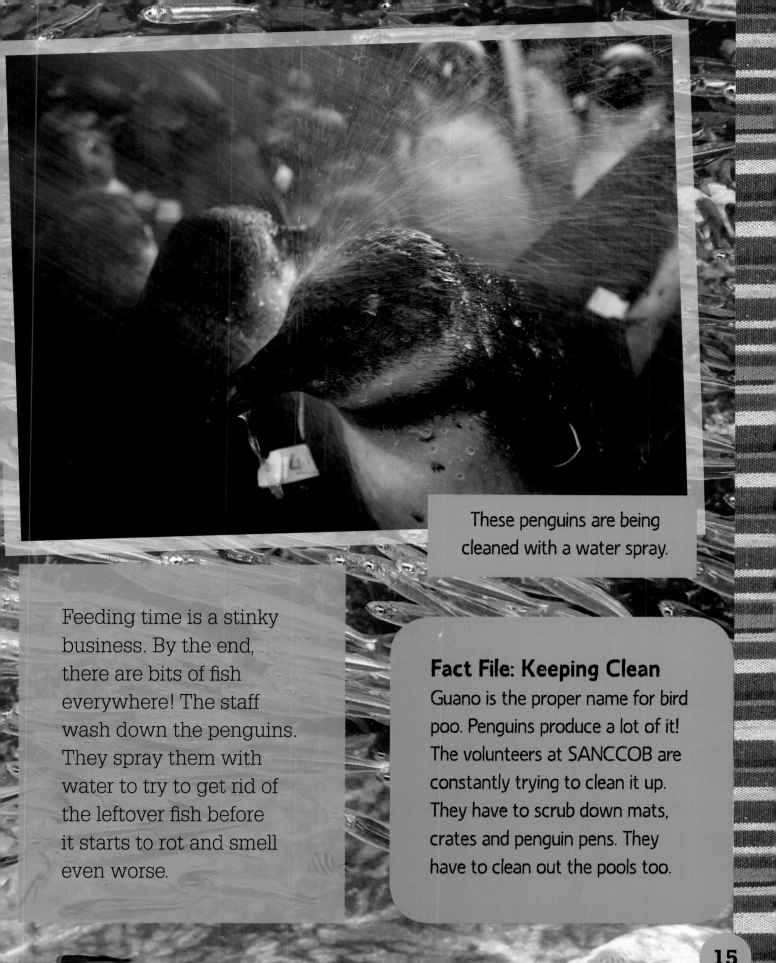

These penguins are being cleaned with a water spray.

Feeding time is a stinky business. By the end, there are bits of fish everywhere! The staff wash down the penguins. They spray them with water to try to get rid of the leftover fish before it starts to rot and smell even worse.

Fact File: Keeping Clean
Guano is the proper name for bird poo. Penguins produce a lot of it! The volunteers at SANCCOB are constantly trying to clean it up. They have to scrub down mats, crates and penguin pens. They have to clean out the pools too.

15

FROM EGG TO CHICK

The rescue centre doesn't only care for chicks and adults. It also finds eggs and does its best to hatch them and raise the chicks. It collects the abandoned eggs from wild colonies.

In the wild, penguin parents keep their eggs at a steady, warm temperature. As soon as an egg is abandoned, it starts to cool off. Hopefully, a warden will find it and transport it to the rescue centre quickly. There, it can be put into an incubator – a machine for keeping eggs or young animals warm. Too much time at a low temperature could affect the growth of the chick inside the egg.

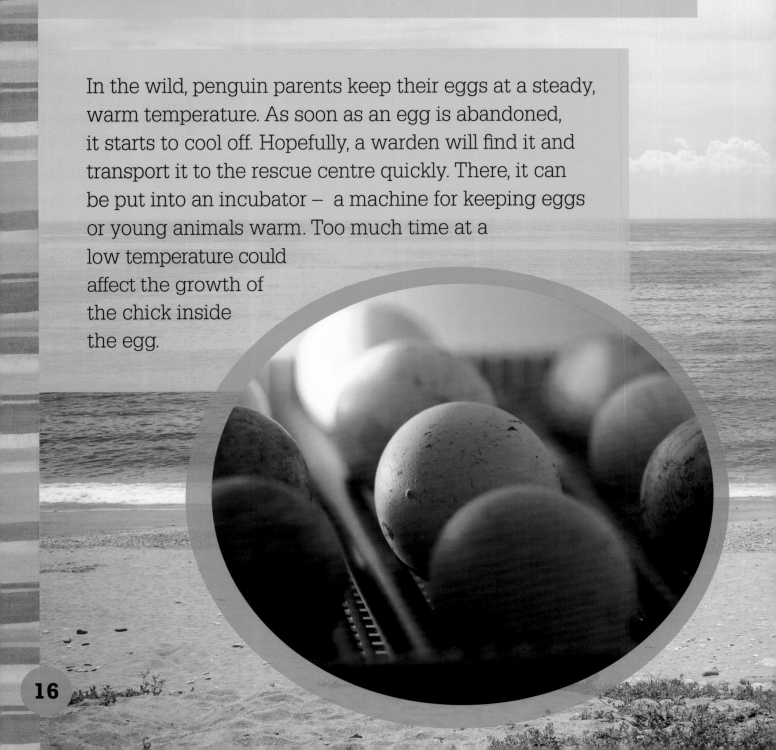

Inside an egg incubator, the air is kept at a steady temperature. The humidity (the dampness of the air) is controlled too. At the first sign of hatching, eggs are moved to a brooder box. The brooder is warmer and more humid than the incubator and has racks so the eggs cannot roll. It can take a chick up to 48 hours to break out of its egg. Afterwards, the chick is moved to the Chick Rearing Unit.

REARING CHICKS

In the Chick Rearing Unit (CRU), staff care for the newly hatched chicks around the clock. They must feed them a droplet of water every hour. They must do the job of penguin parents.

African penguins pair up for life. Each year they produce two eggs. The mum and dad share the job of incubating the eggs. For the first month, they take turns feeding the chicks and keeping them warm. In the CRU, chicks are kept warm under a heat lamp. They snuggle up with a cuddly toy.

Fact File: Chick Crèches

When chicks are a month old, both parents leave them to look for food. The chicks have more chance against gulls and other predators if they stick together in crèches. The chicks stay in the crèches until they grow their adult feathers and can go and catch their own food.

In the wild, penguin parents regurgitate fish (sick it back up) into their chicks' mouths. In the CRU, the staff feed the chicks fish 'milkshake', just like regurgitated fish. It takes patience – the chicks spit out most of their meal, even though they are hungry.

CHICK CHECKS

The **SANCCOB** rescue centre is very good at rearing penguin chicks. That is because it takes care to monitor each individual chick. If a chick is not making enough progress, staff can decide what extra care it needs. Some penguins need care for the rest of their lives.

Occasionally, SANCCOB raise a penguin that has no chance of ever living in the wild. Twinkles hatched with a deformed back. He will never be able to care for himself out at sea, but he has a great life and the staff make a huge fuss of him. Twinkles even has a special harness so staff can take him out for walks.

Chicks at the rescue centre have regular checks from the vet. He or she looks out for some of the common health problems that can affect penguins, such as eye infections or breathing difficulties. The vet uses a stethoscope to listen to the chick's heart and lungs. The chick is also weighed to check that it is gaining weight at the right rate.

RETURN TO THE WILD

In the wild, penguins can fend for themselves from the age of two to four months. At the rescue centre, staff can tell when the birds are ready. They need to be fit, fat and healthy.

The staff use cardboard cargo boxes to transport the birds for release. The boxes have holes so the penguins can breathe. A boat carries the birds out into Table Bay. Once they are far from the shore, the birds are encouraged to leap into the water.

From now on, the penguins will have to fend for themselves. They will have to find and catch their own food. They will also have to avoid predators. Sharks, Cape fur seals and orcas all hunt and eat African penguins.

Fact File: What You Can Do

When people take too many fish from the sea, there is not enough food left for fish-eating sea creatures, such as penguins. This problem is called overfishing. You can help by asking your parents to buy only fish that is described as 'sustainable'. That means that it will not run out.

OTHER BIRDS

Most of SANCCOB's work is with African penguins, but the organisation also looks after other threatened seabirds. Like African penguins, Cape gannets are falling in numbers because of overfishing.

Cape gannets are struggling because there are not enough sardines and anchovies left in the seas around their breeding grounds. The trouble is, the birds always return to the same sites to breed. That means that parents cannot find enough food close to shore to feed themselves and their chicks. Some end up abandoning their chicks and heading out to open waters to feed themselves.

The staff at SANCCOB look after gannet chicks and Hartlaub's gull chicks. They are also good at treating seabird diseases. All the birds SANCCOB save and release are given tags. The tags send back information. Thanks to the tags, they can tell that the birds they have helped are doing well in the wild.

A Hartlaub gull chick is being cared for at SANCCOB.

BLACK DEATH

Pollution is a huge problem for seabirds. They can become tangled up or choke on plastic bags and other rubbish floating in the water. Oil spills also cause serious harm.

Oil spills can have many different causes. A tanker transporting oil may spring a leak. It may have an accident and sink, losing its cargo. The oil in the water clogs up seabirds' feathers. It destroys the natural waterproofing. Without help, the animals will die.

A cape gannet covered in oil from a slick.

Fact File: The Washing Process
To clean a bird, the staff at SANCCOB first cover it with cooking oil. The black oil will stick to this. Then come a series of bubble baths, scrubbing with toothbrushes, and rinses. Finally, the bird dries out under a heat lamp. Its natural waterproofing will recoat its feathers and then it can be set free.

SANCCOB are experts at rescuing oiled birds. First they give the birds a special drink that rehydrates them. It also contains charcoal, which soaks up any oil in their guts. The birds are given antibiotics to stop their eyes becoming infected and other medicine too. Then the long job of washing and rinsing begins.

SPREADING THE WORD

SANCCOB works hard to rescue and rehabilitate seabirds. They also try to make people aware of what is happening. They want everyone to know how important it is to stop overfishing and pollution.

SANCCOB goes into schools to educate teachers and children. The team wants young people to get involved in conservation projects. They take their lucky mascot, Rocky. She is a female rockhopper penguin. She was found far from her colony and could not be returned home. Instead, she helps SANCCOB. She goes into schools and also takes part in other special events.

SANCCOB's research work is important too. It shares its expert knowledge by training students. The students go on to work in other rescue centres around the world. Slowly but surely, SANCCOB is making a difference.

Rocky helping out at a conservation event.

GLOSSARY

ANTIBIOTICS Substances used to treat infectious diseases because they stop bacteria from growing.

COLONY A group of animals of the same species that live closely together.

CONSERVATION Protecting and keeping for the future.

CRUSTACEAN An animal with a shell, for example a crab, lobster or shrimp.

DEHYDRATED Lacking fluids.

ENDANGERED At risk of dying out in the wild forever.

EXTINCTION Disappearing forever.

FORAGE To search for food.

HABITAT The place where an animal or plant lives.

ILLEGAL Against the law.

INCUBATOR A tank that keeps eggs warm until they hatch.

INFECTION A disease or condition caused by germs such as bacteria.

OVERFISHING Taking too many fish from the sea.

PARASITE An animal or plant that survives by living off another animal or plant.

PATROL To travel over an area regularly to check that all is well.

POLLUTION Harmful substances and waste that poison the environment.

PREDATOR An animal that survives by hunting, killing and eating other animals.

REGURGITATE To sick up partly digested food.

REHABILITATE To prepare to live a normal life.

RESERVE An area where the land and its wildlife are being saved for the future.

SPECIES A group of similar organisms that can reproduce together.

SUSTAINABLE Describes an activity that can carry on forever without using up the resources it needs.

VOLUNTEER Someone who works for free.

FURTHER INFORMATION

WEBSITES

pbskids.org/dragonflytv/show/africanpenguins.html
A short film about African penguin behaviour by two workers at the New Jersey State Aquarium, USA.

www.arkive.org/african-penguin/spheniscus-demersus/
Photos and videos of African penguins, plus lots of facts.

www.bbc.co.uk/nature/life/African_Penguin
Information and film clips about African penguins from the BBC.

www.penguins-world.com
Information and pictures of different penguin species, including African penguins.

www.sanccob.co.za
The website of the South African Foundation for the Conservation of Coastal Birds (SANCCOB), which rehabilitates African penguins and other seabirds.

FURTHER READING

100 Facts: Penguins by Camilla de la Bedoyere (Miles Kelly Publishing, 2009)

American Museum of Natural History Easy Readers: Penguins Are Cool! by Peter and Connie Roop (Sterling, 2014)

Discover More: Polar Animals by Susan Hayes and Tory Gordon-Harris (Scholastic, 2014)

National Geographic Readers: Penguins by Anne Schreiber (National Geographic Society, 2009)

Penguins by Valerie Bodden (Franklin Watts, 2012)

Penguins: From Emperors to Macaronis by Erin Pembrey Swan (Franklin Watts, 2003)

INDEX

* Animal Rescue *

SERIES CONTENTS

BAT HOSPITAL

Tolga Bat Hospital • Trouble with Ticks • Tick Treatment • The Nursery • Hospital Workers • Health Check • Preparing Meals • Dinner Time! • The Flight Cage • Foster Care • Return to the Wild • Dangers to Bats • Reaching Out

CHIMP RESCUE

Chimp Sanctuary • Rescuing Chimps • Ngamba Island • Joining the Group • Dinner Time • The Team • Grooming • Human Friendships • Playtime! • Communication • Bedtime • Brainy Behaviour • Reaching Out

ELEPHANT ORPHANS

Elephant Nursery • Threats to Elephants • Mother's Milk • Food Supplies • Dust Baths • A New Arrival • Health Checks • Healing Touch • Elephant Friends • Off for a Walk • Playtime • Bedtime • Spreading the Word

ORANG-UTAN ORPHANS

Saving Orang-Utans • Vanishing Forests • The Pet Trade • Mums and Babies • Carers • Dinner Time • Playtime • Bedtime • Keeping Clean • Being Friendly • Forest Skills • Back to the Wild • Spreading the Word

PANDAS IN DANGER

Panda Centres • Threats to Pandas • A Diet of Bamboo • Breeding Pandas • Newborn Pandas • Feeding Time • Growing Stronger • Better Care • Ready to Explore • Keepers • Playing Outside • Panda Society • Spreading the Word

PENGUIN RESCUE

Saving Seabirds • African Penguins • Chick Rescue • On Arrival • Daily Routine • Dinner Time • From Egg to Chick • Rearing Chicks • Chick Checks • Return to the Wild • Other Birds • Black Death • Spreading the Word